For me, the phrase "TELL ME" always represents an invitation. For my readers, I invite you to "TELL ME" your perspectives as we try to make health care better in a difficult world. Join me at https://aha.pub/TELLME and become part of a great community dedicated to transformational changes in health care!

Doc Philip Brown

—Doc Philip Brown

Do You Speak Patient?

An Actionable Journal for Credible Medical Professionals

Doc Philip Brown

Foreword by Charles J. Hardy, PhD

E-mail: info@thinkaha.com
20660 Stevens Creek Blvd., Suite 210
Cupertino, CA 95014

Please go to
https://aha.pub/DoYouSpeakPatient
to read this AHAbook and to share the
individual AHA messages that resonate with you.

_AHA_that˙

Published by THiNKaha®
20660 Stevens Creek Blvd., Suite 210,
Cupertino, CA 95014
https://thinkaha.com
E-mail: **info@thinkaha.com**

THiNK_aha_˙

First Printing: March 2023
Hardcover ISBN: 978-1-61699-399-3 1-61699-399-5
Paperback ISBN: 978-1-61699-398-6 1-61699-398-7
eBook ISBN: 978-1-61699-397-9 1-61699-397-9
Place of Publication: Silicon Valley, California, USA
Paperback Library of Congress Number: 2022917916

All proceeds of the book will go to fund an endowed scholarship for health professions students at the University of North Carolina Wilmington called the "HEALTH EQUITY FOR ASPIRING LEADERS SCHOLARSHIP," also known as the HEAL Scholarship.

Dedication

This book is dedicated in loving memory of my mother-in-law, Willow Dean Blackmon. Having her at home with my family during her last months of life gave me a new understanding of what care really is, and what the medical care system needs to be. For that, I am forever grateful.

Acknowledgements

I would like to acknowledge the sacrifices made by my family during my career as a physician. I fear too often that the sense of responsibility for the lives of patients demanded a disproportionate amount of my time, which could only then be taken from my wife Christy, son Philip, and daughter Sallie. I am grateful to them for enriching my life and for the love and support that saw me through very stressful times.

To my parents Mike and Bonnie Brown, thank you for the foundation of the person I continue to become. My sense of duty and service came from you, and it has helped many patients along this journey. I also appreciate your steadfast support throughout the years.

To my brother David Brown and sister Karrie Rushing, thank you for always being there. While the demands of the profession may have created physical and emotional distance, there has never been a question about the closeness of our bond. I have always known that you are there in times of need, at most a phone call away.

To the many teachers, professors, and mentors over the years, thank you for sharing your gifts in ways that allowed me to develop my own to pass along to others. You may have been formal or informal instructors, and I feel so blessed to have always been surrounded by people doing their best to help others, while helping me learn and become a better physician. Some of you may not even be aware of how positively you affected me, and I hope you come to know how much I appreciate it.

To my colleagues through the years, thank you for tolerating and supporting me in tough times, and for sharing with me the joys of helping others. I have found no substitute for the unwritten understanding between medical professionals, whether it be about saving a life or being helpless to stop disease and death.

Finally, to those patients who entrusted me your care, thank you for adding such meaning to my life, for being a true partner in your health, and for believing I would always do my best for you.

How to Read a THiNKaha® Book
A Note from the Publisher

The AHAthat/THiNKaha series was crafted to deliver content the way humans process information in today's world—short, sweet, and to the point, while delivering powerful, lasting impact.

The content is designed and presented to appeal to visual, auditory, and kinesthetic personality types. Each section contains AHA messages, lines for notes, and a meme that summarizes that section. You should also scan the QR code or click on the link to watch a video of the author talking about that section.

This book is contextual in nature. Although the words won't change, their meaning will every time you read it, just as your context will. Be ready, you will experience your own AHA moments as you read. The AHA messages are designed to be stand-alone actionable messages that will help you think differently. Items to consider as you're reading include:

1. It should only take less than an hour to read the first time. When you're reading, write one to three action items that resonate with you in the underlined areas.
2. Mark your calendar to re-read it again.
3. Repeat step #1 and mark one to three additional AHA messages that resonate. As they will most likely be different, this is a great time to reflect on the messages that resonated with you during your last reading.
4. Sprinkle credust on the author and yourself by sharing the AHA messages from this book socially from the AHAthat platform https://aha.pub/DoYouSpeakPatient.

After reading this THiNKaha book, marking your AHA messages, rereading it, and marking more AHA messages, you'll begin to see how this book contextually applies to you. We advocate for continuous, lifelong learning, and this book will help you transform your AHAs into action items with tangible results.

Mitchell Levy, Global Credibility Expert
publisher@thinkaha.com

A THiNKaha book is not your typical book. It's a whole lot more, while being a whole lot less. Scan the QR code or use this link to watch me talk about this new evolutionary style of book: https://aha.pub/THiNKahaSeries

Contents

Foreword

In *Do You Speak Patient: An Actionable Journal for Credible Medical Professionals*, Dr. Philip Brown has created a practical roadmap for those who are committed to enhancing the health and quality of life of individuals, families, and communities. The AHAthat/THINKaha format of this book is intended to be used as an actionable journal for the reader. The section summaries are brief and are followed by a series of "AHA points" presented in a format to allow the reader to reflect and add their perspective.

This approach allows the author to deliver the content with high impact in a direct and pointed manner, as well as to invite the reader to contribute to the dialogue through reflection and journaling to specific prompts/questions. Such an approach is refreshing and powerful, demanding both consumption and production.

This readable and imminently useful book builds on and expands the AHAthat/THINKaha model of self-reflection through journaling to health care. Dr. Brown presents a model that has helped him reconnect to his purpose as a physician – "TELL ME." This acronym (Trust, Empathy, Listening, Limiting Constraints, Maintaining Health, and Eliminating Barriers) provides the cornerstone for the different sections of this book.

Following the summaries of each of the elements of TELL ME in separate sections of the book, the author challenges the reader to add their own thoughts and feelings to an inventory of penetrating questions/statements connected to each element of the model. Through this process, the author invites the reader to reflect, think, and share their values, training, and real-life experiences to each element of the acronym. The author states that "*as that happens, it is my hope that your sense of purpose can be refueled in meaningful ways, that you can find ways to ignite others, and that we all move a little closer to understanding how much we count on each other for health and quality of life as we strive to help each other through the most difficult life challenges.*"

This book is intended to be an active experience. Clearly, the more you put into reading and contributing to this book, the more you will gain. While a quick read will take about an hour, providing your own responses to the reflective questions/comments for each element in the TELL ME model is, and was intended to be, a lifelong experience. The book is also connected to a social platform – the AHAthat platform https://aha.pub/DoYouSpeakPatient – for you to share your AHA messages with others.

The goal of this book experience is to help the reader transform AHAs into actionable items with tangible results toward a better state of health for individuals, families, and communities. Through this process, the author hopes to move health care to a more interdependent model where professionals are driven by TELL ME, where personal and collective values and expectations of their patients and themselves result in a team approach to health and wellness. It should be noted that the author has committed the proceeds from this book to providing financial assistance to students enrolled in health programs at the University of North Carolina Wilmington through the Health Equity for Aspiring Leaders (HEAL) Endowed Scholarship – this TELLS ME that Dr. Brown is committed to igniting others to overcome difficult life challenges by connecting to his own sense of purpose as a healthcare professional.

Charles J. Hardy, PhD
Professor and Founding Dean
College of Health and Human Services
University of North Carolina Wilmington

Introduction

Why join the medical profession in the first place? For many medical professionals, the drive is a powerful desire to conquer disease combined with a solemn covenant to care for people — fellow human beings — to the best of one's abilities and judgments. This sense of purpose combined with the fulfillment obtained through complex problem solving becomes a powerful motivator that allows one to push the limits of personal growth during education and training.

After medical school, residency training, and fellowship, or one of the many educational tracks in health care, professionals set out to deliver quality health care, often with inadequate early mentorship. Then somewhere along the way, the burning passion and motivation that initially provided all the energy necessary to make a difference in the lives of others gets replaced with a sense of frustration and futility. Once this pattern emerges, the template for personal trauma is in place. Until that pattern is interrupted, the risk to both professional and patient is on an escalating trend line. Danger is near.

I wish I could claim to have THE answer, a single path forward to navigate away from the abyss. But the truth is much more modest. What I do have is a simple mental model that has helped me reconnect to purpose. I am going to share it with you in the hope that your version will help you. For me, when I think back to all the patient visits that began with me saying, "TELL ME," the acronym takes me directly to that sense of purpose. You see, "TELL ME" was always an invitation. "TELL ME how things are going," or "TELL ME what brings you in today" provided a powerful opening for my patient to talk, and for me to listen. The connection soon followed, yet "TELL ME" has always been the start. In this short book, I will explain what "TELL ME" has come to represent for me.

T is for trust - the foundation of relationship between professionals and patients.
E is for empathy - the ability to truly see from another's perspective.
L is for listen - the only path to know what the patient wants and hopes for their care.
L is for limit constraints - only by understanding them first are we able to successfully navigate them.
M is for maintain health - the easier path to wellness is to go forward and not to take steps backward.
E is for eliminate barriers - some barriers to care can't be worked around, they must be removed.

The acronym is simple, but not always easy to do. As we go through each chapter, I will highlight some of the "AHA" moments that have occurred to me during my career. It is my hope that these simple representations will stimulate thinking so that you are able to attach your career experiences to the framework. As that happens, it is my hope that your sense of purpose can be refueled in meaningful ways, that you can find ways to ignite others, and that we all move a little closer to understanding how much we count on each other for health and quality of life as we strive to help others overcome their most difficult life challenges. And of course, as has always been the case, "TELL ME" is just a beginning.

Share the AHA messages from this book socially by going to
https://aha.pub/DoYouSpeakPatient

Scan the QR code or use this link to watch the section videos and more on this section topic:
https://aha.pub/DoYouSpeakPatientSVs

Section I

Introduction

As medical professionals, we strive to deliver our best care to patients. In so doing, it is important to remember that patients are human beings, not just medical data on a chart. Confusion at this point may result in a mismatch of expectations between patient and caregiver.

The basic foundation of our profession is to "care" for our fellow humans. Without truly caring for others, we may fail to provide the quality health care they deserve due to our own ignorance of what they value. In other terms, we must know them before we care for them.

It is also of critical importance that our patients know we care about them. If they don't, how will all the training we've gone through or the certifications we've earned make us trustworthy to them? Remember, they're entrusting us with their lives. Patients want to know, see, and feel that the medical professionals they're entrusting their lives with truly care about them. Anything short of that is insufficient.

Aside from caring about the patient, we also need to care about the patient's support system. How we treat the patient's family, friends, and loved ones should be consistent with the kind of compassion deserved by people facing the major life stress of helping a loved one through a severe life challenge.

This section provides a premise for the entire book on how we, medical professionals, can make patients' lives better by caring enough about them to understand their health desires and support structures, and by engaging them as co-creators in the plan to survive their challenge and reach their highest level of health.

Whether you're a doctor, nurse, technologist, or any member of the healthcare team, this book will help you rediscover your passion to help people. It will also help you reignite your belief and motivation that the medical profession is a higher calling than perhaps any other career on earth.

1

As a medical professional, it is important to remember that patients are human beings, not just numerical data on a chart. #CredibleMedicalProfessional

_____

_____

_____

2

The motivation for many medical professionals to enter the field is to make people's lives easier and better. What other factors inspire you to stay in health care? #CredibleMedicalProfessional

_____

_____

_____

3

Nobody cares how much you know until they know how much you care. What ways do you show how much you care? #CredibleMedicalProfessional

_____

_____

_____

4

Credibility in the medical field requires caring about and caring for people. What makes it difficult for you to show how much you care about a certain patient or group? #CredibleMedicalProfessional

_____

_____

_____

5

Medical professionals should have the skills, good judgment, and manners expected of someone who's well trained to deliver quality health care. What's your greatest strength and which of these domains needs the most effort? #CredibleMedicalProfessional

_____

_____

6

Table stakes for credible medical professionals are training, initial board certification, and reputable practice. Patients will only trust you more when they know you care about them. #CredibleMedicalProfessional

_____

_____

_____

7

Patients, friends, and family will ask for your recommendation. Sometimes they don't need textbook answers, but rather the assurance that you actually care. How do you listen with that in mind? #CredibleMedicalProfessional

_____

_____

_____

8

Honoring the patient's health desires can sometimes outweigh specific techniques for disease management. Listen to understand, it gives the best chance to make the right recommendation. #CredibleMedicalProfessional

_____

_____

_____

9

When you know that someone cares for you, you love the person back. That agape love patients have with medical professionals is key to being and staying healthy. #CredibleMedicalProfessional

---

10

Medical professionals are almost like extensions of family with the level of care that they provide to patients. That relationship is crucial for the patient to transition from sickness to good health. #CredibleMedicalProfessional

_____

_____

_____

11

Medical professionals deliver quality care by caring for their patients with the passion they would their own family, but consistent with the values of the patient and their supports. #CredibleMedicalProfessional

_____

_____

_____

12

Value not just the patient, but also their support system by setting expectations, communicating, and demonstrating how much you care. #CredibleMedicalProfessional

_____

_____

_____

13

Treat the patient's support system - their family, friends, and loved ones - just like you would treat the patient. #CredibleMedicalProfessional

_____

_____

_____

14

The medical profession is not just a job; it is a higher calling to serve people. Your patients are fellow humans who deserve love and respect. Treat them consistently with what they value. #TheCrediblePhysican

_____

_____

_____

Share the AHA messages from this book socially by going to
https://aha.pub/DoYouSpeakPatient

Scan the QR code or use this link to watch the section videos and more on this section topic:
https://aha.pub/DoYouSpeakPatientSVs

Section II

Trust is the Foundation

Without a relationship built on trust, medical professionals have little chance of creating the right healing environment for patients. Deep trust occurs soon after the patient and their supports make the leap of understanding that their medical professional not only cares about managing their disease, but, more importantly, about the patient's personal well-being.

The most important concept in this book is described by this paradox: While the medical professional is an authority in applying his/her expertise and knowledge on diseases and treatments, it is the patient who has the authority to make decisions for his/her own health. This paradox can only be perfectly reconciled when there is clear bi-directional communication between professional and patient. Simply stated, the patient or their delegate always has decision rights. To a significant extent, there can be a process of discovery that leads to co-creation of care plans. When things happen this way, there is a much greater chance of adherence to the plan. Patient buy-in is built in from the beginning. Ultimately, this is the condition required for a healthy relationship between patient and healthcare professional.

15

As medical professionals, trust is one of the most effective ways to get patients and their support system on board to better the patient's well-being. #DoYouSpeakPatient

_____

_____

_____

16

There's a paradox of authority in patient relationships. The medical professional is the authority on disease, but the patient has the decision rights for their care. We need to build trust to provide the best quality care. #DoYouSpeakPatient

_____

_____

_____

17

An intimate bond forms when patients trust their medical team. It's a meaningful relationship, especially for patients, because it makes their lives better. It also fulfills the medical professional. #DoYouSpeakPatient

_____

_____

_____

18

To build patient trust, communication has to be effective and bi-directional between the medical professional and the patient. #DoYouSpeakPatient

_____

_____

_____

19

If the communication pathways are open enough, even if patients sense change, they will seek you out immediately. Are you available and accessible to your patient? #DoYouSpeakPatient

_____

_____

_____

20

Patients often ask for the medical professional's personal opinion, but until you share a common set of values, your recommendations may be interpreted skeptically. #DoYouSpeakPatient

_____

_____

_____

21

Medical professionals need to understand what the patient's health desires and values are -- the guiding compass in explaining what their options will be in terms of their treatment plan. #DoYouSpeakPatient

_____

_____

_____

22

Before doing any procedure, you need to be able to explain what your patient can expect from both their experience and yours, and what the chances are in terms of outcomes. #DoYouSpeakPatient

_____

_____

_____

23

Are you talking to your patient about the physical probabilities of risk in a language that they can understand? It's important not to confuse them with medical jargon. #DoYouSpeakPatient

---

24

There are times when medical professionals will need to make a more authoritative decision and tell the patient that a certain procedure can't be done safely for them, or must be done to maximize their chances. #DoYouSpeakPatient

---

25

How hard is it to admit that not all interventions help patients get better? Where do you draw the line on candor? #DoYouSpeakPatient

_____

_____

_____

26

It takes a lot of courage to make difficult decisions about patient care. How do you compassionately convey to a patient's family that you are concerned the patient won't make it? #DoYouSpeakPatient

_____

_____

_____

27

After making a mutual decision on a treatment plan with your patient, give it a chance to work. You and the plan lose credibility if medical professionals incite doubt in patients and their support system once the plan is decided. #DoYouSpeakPatient

_____

_____

_____

28

Every new treatment represents a significant change
for a person, including long-term behavior changes.
To make that step, you need to get their buy-in first.
#DoYouSpeakPatient

_____

_____

_____

29

Some patients may not be compliant and will give you
answers they think you'd want to hear regarding their
treatment. It's important to get their honest opinion and
buy-in on what's next for them. #DoYouSpeakPatient

_____

_____

_____

30

Patient commitment to a plan is more likely when you understand and clearly express what's most important to them, so they say, "That's right." If they say, "You're right," there's likely more understanding to be developed. #DoYouSpeakPatient

_____

_____

_____

31

The patient's recovery will be compromised if they don't really believe in or agree with your suggested course of action. #DoYouSpeakPatient

_____

_____

_____

32

Patients go to the medical professional whom they trust will do the best job of addressing what they have. Are you worthy of their trust? #DoYouSpeakPatient

_____

_____

_____

33

Do you speak "patient?" When you know your patient enough, you better understand what they need and want. In return, your patient and their support system will be more cooperative. #DoYouSpeakPatient

_____

_____

_____

34

As a medical professional, it's your responsibility to ensure that your patient understands that they're in a safe environment to express their true feelings and pain. #DoYouSpeakPatient

_____

_____

_____

35

Most patients walking into a doctor's office are scared. After seeing that they are in a safe environment, they'll feel better and more comfortable. #DoYouSpeakPatient

_____

_____

_____

Share the AHA messages from this book socially by going to
https://aha.pub/DoYouSpeakPatient

Scan the QR code or use this link to watch the section videos and more on this section topic:
https://aha.pub/DoYouSpeakPatientSVs

Section III

Empathy Creates Context

As a medical professional, expressing empathy toward patients and their support systems is a head start for delivering excellent care. It creates an understanding between you and your patients that you truly care about them.

Patients need to know that they matter and that their lives are valued. Thus, medical professionals need to honor the patients' health desires in a way that they can recognize -- so that their treatment plan really improves their health and makes them better.

At the end of the day, the right end result in treating patients revolves around understanding exactly what their health desires are, and providing a safe care environment for them and their support system to move toward that outcome. We need to listen to and empathize with the patients and their loved ones.

The whole support system around that patient, such as family and friends, needs to know that the entire team of medical professionals looking after their loved one is really advocating for what's best for the patient.

This section talks about how medical professionals can deliver quality health care with empathy, and how empathy enables patients to commit to getting optimal health.

36

The expression of a medical professional's empathy to a patient and their colleagues creates an alliance, which assures the patient that you care about them. What expressions of empathy towards colleagues are most memorable? #LiveWithEmpathy

_____

_____

_____

37

As a medical professional, you need good judgment to deliver quality health care. Good judgment requires empathy and knowing your patient's values and support system. #LiveWithEmpathy

_____

_____

_____

38

Good judgment comes from experience, and experience often comes from bad judgment. You learn from years of education and practice. Which real-life, bad judgment calls have you learned not to repeat? #LiveWithEmpathy

_____

_____

_____

39

Executing changes with the patient is no easy task. How do you use empathy to help make the changed plan work? #LiveWithEmpathy

_____

_____

_____

40

When patients ask you, "What would you do if you were in my position?" an empathetic approach is more likely to lead to sound advice. How do you demonstrate this? #LiveWithEmpathy

_____

_____

_____

41

Whatever course of treatment you recommend should be grounded through an understanding of what's important to your patients. #LiveWithEmpathy

_____

_____

_____

42

Navigating change for a patient, a fellow human being, at what could be one of the worst times in their life is crucial. To do what's right by the patient, empathize with their total situation. #LiveWithEmpathy

_____

_____

_____

43

Help your patients feel better in a way that they recognize. Even in end-of-life care, they can experience what quality of life is about! #LiveWithEmpathy

_____

_____

_____

44

Getting the patient and the medical professional on the same page is both difficult and important. How do you create alignment? #LiveWithEmpathy

_____

_____

_____

45

Sometimes the compassionate thing to do in end-of-life care is for medical professionals to acknowledge their own vulnerability by admitting to a patient and family that nothing effective can be done to cure the illness. #LiveWithEmpathy

---

46

Saying to a family, "We did everything we could," can be easier than saying, "I wish there was something we could do," which requires courageous humility. But the easier way leads to futile care and can be more painful to the family. #LiveWithEmpathy

---

47

Medical professionals should become skilled
at explaining things to people in ways they
can understand. Simplify medical terminology.
#LiveWithEmpathy

_____

_____

_____

48

Doing what's right by the patient requires effectively communicating patient care plans and ensuring that the patient commits to their treatment process. #LiveWithEmpathy

_____

_____

_____

49

Medical professionals need to empathize with the patient and gain their trust to enable them to make a sound choice about their health. #LiveWithEmpathy

_____

_____

_____

50

It is important to communicate the care process and actively listen to the patient. Empathy can remove the patient's doubt, which often hinders their commitment to a treatment plan. #LiveWithEmpathy

_____

_____

_____

51

Patient compliance is less effective than patient commitment. Patients only commit to treatment suggestions when they are achievable for them and consistent with their best interest for optimal health. #LiveWithEmpathy

---

52

Empathy strengthens the connection and loyalty between the medical professional and the patient so that both are committed to the long-term improvement and maintenance of health. #LiveWithEmpathy

---

Share the AHA messages from this book socially by going to
https://aha.pub/DoYouSpeakPatient

Scan the QR code or use this link to watch the section videos and more on this section topic:
https://aha.pub/DoYouSpeakPatientSVs

Section IV

Listen with Deep Curiosity

Doctor-patient relationships are more about understanding the patient and their desired quality of life than about treating disease, and the same is true about relationships between all healthcare professionals and patients. That's why it's important for medical professionals to be skilled listeners, so that they are able to maintain a healthy relationship with their colleagues and patients.

When quality patient care is delivered in an environment characterized by mutual trust and respect, the bond created is very strong. The level of mutual commitment creates excellent conditions for successful treatment and recovery. In many cases, the reciprocal bonds of trust create conditions similar to those found in a close family, where deep caring and love are dominant emotions. Under these conditions, authentic curiosity is a powerful stimulus to listen deeply. This type of listening is a common challenge for healthcare professions, because training and environmental conditions have fostered a mentality of "racing to the right answer" for diagnosis and treatment. The risk from such an approach is an inadequate understanding of personal patient factors. This often leads to misguided action, ranging from poor communication to fatal clinical error.

53

Patient care isn't limited to just treating disease, but also to helping the patient reach their desired quality of life. #CredibleMedicalProfessional

_____

_____

_____

54

A powerful patient relationship gives the patient the best chances of going from sickness to health. #CredibleMedicalProfessional

_____

_____

_____

55

There's power in listening. Some patients may struggle to articulate their pain and struggles. As medical professionals, you'll learn to pick up on cues to hear what they do and do not say. #DoYouSpeakPatient

_____

_____

_____

56

William Osler, a famous internal medicine physician at Johns Hopkins, said, "Listen to your patient -- he is telling you the diagnosis!" It's your job to listen first. #DoYouSpeakPatient

_____

_____

_____

57

Evidence-based medical protocols can become risky when not consistent with the patient's health desires and values. Listen closely to the patient because context is decisive. #CredibleMedicalProfessional

---

58

If the patient relationship becomes transactional, it's a recipe for reduced outcomes and non-compliance. #CredibleMedicalProfessional

---

59

A strong relationship that includes the patient and the patient's support system can boost confidence in the course of action being recommended by medical professionals. #CredibleMedicalProfessional

---

60

Your guidance in keeping patients safe is supported by a strong and healthy relationship with them that can result in faster recovery and healing. #CredibleMedicalProfessional

---

61

Patients submit themselves to a covenant of care with medical professionals to improve their health. It's a kind of intimacy in the profession that is honored through empathy and respect. #CredibleMedicalProfessional

_____

_____

_____

62

Both the medical professional and the patient benefit from being in a healthy relationship anchored in the foundation of deep and mutual respect. That's where everything starts! #CredibleMedicalProfessional

_____

_____

_____

63

The mutual respect and relationship between medical professionals and patients positively impact health outcomes. #CredibleMedicalProfessional

_____

_____

_____

64

Successfully building a patient relationship takes time and effort, so don't stress about it happening overnight. Start with trust in your bedside manner and you will be more likely to get trust in return. #CredibleMedicalProfessional

---

65

Developing and maintaining good relationships with your patients means being compassionate and mindful, as they may be scared and confused. Reassure them and show that you really care! #CredibleMedicalProfessional

---

66

Helping a patient and their support system successfully navigate through changes in the patient's treatment plan happens when the medical professional maintains a good relationship with the patient. #CredibleMedicalProfessional

_____

_____

_____

67

Encourage change when it needs to happen to foster good relationships and produce favorable health outcomes. This could significantly transform a patient's life! #CredibleMedicalProfessional

_____

_____

_____

68

Your patients will feel more comfortable with you during each encounter because they trust, know, and love you! #CredibleMedicalProfessional

_____

_____

_____

69

Many patients actually love the medical professionals they work with. A deep bond develops when your patient trusts you with their life. #CredibleMedicalProfessional

_____

_____

_____

70

The medical professional-patient relationship is associated with an incredible expression of trust, which overflows to the entire ecosystem for patient care to be successful. #CredibleMedicalProfessional

_____

_____

_____

71

A patient relationship built on trust fosters mutual commitment to the treatment plan and to changes that will impact the patient's quality of life. #CredibleMedicalProfessional

_____

_____

_____

Share the AHA messages from this book socially by going to
https://aha.pub/DoYouSpeakPatient

Scan the QR code or use this link to watch the section videos and more on this section topic:
https://aha.pub/DoYouSpeakPatientSVs

Section V

Limit Constraints Together

Credible medical professionals are committed to providing outstanding care and service to patients. When held back from this deep-seated desire, it is common for the professional to experience distress. Recognition of this phenomenon leads one to the possibility of a constraint in care. Simply defined, a constraint is a limitation or restriction. So when this happens in care, the professional often becomes frustrated. In patient care, constraints are multifactorial, potentially arising from patient factors, caregiver factors, provider factors, and system factors.

In order to make sure outstanding care is delivered, the first step is to recognize the existence of a constraint. Simply stated, the immediate question becomes, "What is limiting the execution of this plan?" Up to now, we have developed trust, shown empathy, and listened with curiosity. Our planning should be set up for success, but somehow it isn't working. How do we understand the cause of the constraint?

Working through categories is a solid approach at this point. The first point of curiosity when it seems a patient is unable or unwilling to follow a plan is always to ask oneself if all the patient factors were well understood. One of the most common and insidious constraints occurs when there is an expectation mismatch between the patient and the medical professional.

We can revisit empathy and listening to answer this question. Commonly there has been a near miss or a total misunderstanding of what the patient can accomplish given their support system and beliefs. This phenomenon underscores the essential nature of co-creating solutions (remember the paradox of care, AHA #16).

If this is not the case, we can shift our interrogation to provider factors and system factors as the culprit. Was the expectation matched but the explanation unclear? Were we all aligned with regard to how to meet expectations? Are there competing interests for factors necessary to the execution of this plan? System constraints in health care are very common, based primarily on how to navigate the utilization of scarce resources by multiple stakeholders of different backgrounds. This is rarely diabolical, but is frequently detrimental. Navigating these system constraints in a manner that is fair and just for all stakeholders is difficult, especially given time pressure and its effects on the triage of patients based on acuity.

Delivering safe, high-quality patient care despite the presence of system constraints represents one of the greatest challenges in health care. Even when we are facing extreme challenges within the medical profession, we must keep going. Patients treated by medical professionals who are able to effectively deal with constraints have higher chances of recovering good health. It is incumbent upon all to continually focus on eliminating a mismatch of treatment plan and patient expectation. We can only reach the pinnacle of patient care when all constraints are eliminated. This requires a firm understanding of patient factors that may constrain the execution of a given care plan. Consistent efforts led by those at the frontlines of care must be made to promote optimal environments of care, in the interest of both team member and patient safety and well-being.

This page is intentionally left blank.

72

As a medical professional, your reputation and capability are often affected by challenges and limitations. Are you available, affable, and able? These are the three A's that make a #CredibleMedicalProfessional!

_____

_____

_____

73

If you feel like your profession is veering you away from your purpose, it's highly likely that there are constraints getting in your way. Where do you find obstacles to giving quality care? #CredibleMedicalProfessional

_____

_____

_____

74

Medical professionals need health checks, too. Physical and mental breaks can help in productivity and efficiency. How do you engage your team to develop alternative solutions despite many constraints? #CredibleMedicalProfessional

---

75

Constraints and possibilities intersect in the life of a medical professional. In helping restore your patient's health, how do you turn constraints into possibilities to reduce stress? #CredibleMedicalProfessional

---

76

The medical professional is always ranked as a high stress career. How do we assure the stress does not impair quality care and patient safety? #CredibleMedicalProfessional

_____

_____

_____

77

Transmitting your own stress onto another team member is counterproductive. Be respectful and kind to one another. We are all vulnerable and commonly willing to help one another. #CredibleMedicalProfessional

_____

_____

_____

78

If medical professionals continue to be scarce due to unnecessary stress, who will assume the responsibility of restoring health? #CredibleMedicalProfessional

_____

_____

_____

79

Unmanaged constraints often lead to negative behavior. When do you go on survival mode, where you may be prone to errors and poor quality of patient care? #CredibleMedicalProfessional

_____

_____

_____

80

Medical professionals need to manage
constraints to continue to be effective caretakers.
#CredibleMedicalProfessionals know how to manage
constraints well. What are your key tactics?

_____

_____

_____

81

Influence and negotiation skills come in handy for medical professionals, especially when faced with difficult decisions and external pressure.
#CredibleMedicalProfessional

_____

_____

_____

82

Medical professionals have patients waiting to use the facilities, which means there are delays. How do you address these waiting periods, as they may have consequences for the patient?
#CredibleMedicalProfessional

_____

_____

_____

83

Medical professionals who involve patients in a shared decision-making process can improve outcomes and reduce costs, which ultimately avoids unnecessary admission/readmission and inefficient use of resources. #CredibleMedicalProfessional

_____

_____

_____

84

Resource utilization in the healthcare system can be tedious and challenging. Medical professionals should have the tools to provide care, which is especially crucial in life-saving situations. #CredibleMedicalProfessional

---

85

Dealing with constraints is often a matter of life or death. Medical professionals need strong system support when dealing with patients' lack of insurance and financial challenges. What're your sources of system support? #CredibleMedicalProfessional

---

86

Medical professionals recognize that even financial constraints and communication barriers shouldn't prevent patients from getting the care they deserve and need. How does your system enable inclusive care? #CredibleMedicalProfessional

_____

_____

_____

87

Medical professionals who successfully navigate constraints remove the consequences of putting patients at risk of harm. #CredibleMedicalProfessional

_____

_____

_____

88

Patients cared for by medical professionals capable of dealing with constraints have higher chances of returning to health. #CredibleMedicalProfessional

_____

_____

_____

Share the AHA messages from this book socially by going to
https://aha.pub/DoYouSpeakPatient

Scan the QR code or use this link to watch the section videos and more on this section topic:
https://aha.pub/DoYouSpeakPatientSVs

Section VI

Maintain Health. It is More Effective Than Restoring It

Preventive medicine is one of the ways in which we, medical professionals, can help address patients' healthcare needs before they become even bigger concerns.

Before reaching the last line of defense against poor health, medical professionals need to understand what drives health outcomes and their impact on patients and the world.

Medical professionals can learn how to assess different factors that produce different health outcomes. Before health is compromised, there are patterns called social drivers of health that make massive differences in health potential for given individuals or groups.

For example, health behaviors such as diet and exercise or drug and alcohol use are often dictated by where patients live, work, learn, and play. Moreover, social and economic factors such as employment, community safety, and education can either expose them to trauma or not. Air and water quality, housing conditions, and modes of transit may also contribute to diminishing health.

In this section, we will talk about how medical professionals need to recognize these things in order to establish a deeper understanding of the true risk factors for and obstacles to good health. Often this understanding requires close communication among the healthcare team, because patients have varying degrees of comfort about who to disclose this information to.

Remember that a whole lot of open communication and encouragement happens here. Medical professionals, patients and their support systems, and hospital staff need to be in alignment to effectively onboard everyone to better the patient's health.

89

Preventive medicine helps encourage patients to talk about their health concerns before bigger issues arise. There is no room for shortcuts or easy fixes when it comes to health. #CredibleMedicalProfessional

---

90

Lots of medical battles are fought around the last line of defense. Early detection is better. If they had been caught ahead of time, the big battles may have been avoided. #CredibleMedicalProfessional

---

91

Medical professionals need to be able to detect early warning signals. Dealing with health problems early on can avoid setting the patients up for risky situations. #CredibleMedicalProfessional

_____

_____

_____

92

Medical professionals need to understand what drives health outcomes and their impact on patients. When they know what to look for, patients won't need to reach their health's last line of defense. #CredibleMedicalProfessional

_____

_____

_____

93

Some health outcomes may require more complex assessments. Before all health is lost, recommend clinical care to provide specific measures before and after treatment. #CredibleMedicalProfessional

_____

_____

_____

94

Some patients may require more immediate care than others. Medical professionals need to think on their feet about the need for emergency care. #CredibleMedicalProfessional

_____

_____

_____

95

When emergent care becomes necessary, achieving good outcomes becomes more difficult, and ready access to medical professionals is critical. #CredibleMedicalProfessional

_____

_____

_____

96

Medical professionals need to be able to help patients see the early success of recommended treatment plans and preventive maintenance for them to be onboard with the recommendation. #CredibleMedicalProfessional

_____

_____

_____

97

Medical professionals should consider socioeconomic factors, health behaviors, physical environment, and clinical care as factors that drive health outcomes. #CredibleMedicalProfessional

_____

_____

_____

98

See if a patient lives in safe housing or not. A sound preventive maintenance plan could mean improving a patient's living conditions by removing hazards around them. #CredibleMedicalProfessional

_____

_____

_____

99

Does your patient have access to healthy food options? Are there parks nearby for the patient to walk and exercise in? Oftentimes, a patient's physical environment shapes their health outcomes. #CredibleMedicalProfessional

---

100

Medical professionals should encourage healthy behaviors to improve a patient's quality of life. #CredibleMedicalProfessional

---

101

What habits do your patients need to keep them safe?
You need to help them commit to what can make
them functional in the environment that they live in.
#CredibleMedicalProfessional

_____

_____

_____

102

Change leadership is important in communicating
changes, not only to patients, but to everyone involved
in patient care, including hospital staff and the patient's
support system. #CredibleMedicalProfessional

_____

_____

_____

103

Medical professionals should learn to assess where patients choose to spend their time and resources. Do the patient's behaviors cost them their life in the long term? #CredibleMedicalProfessional

_____

_____

_____

104

Medical professionals, hospital staff, patients, and their support systems need to be in alignment to effectively onboard everyone into a holistic approach to the patient's health. #CredibleMedicalProfessional

_____

_____

_____

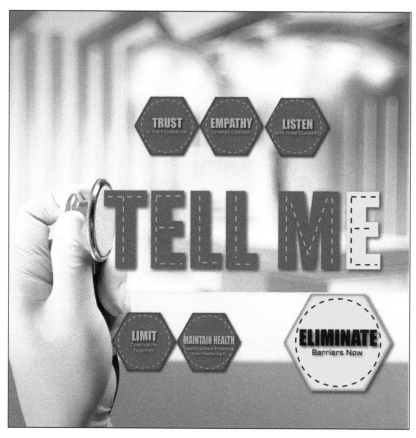

Share the AHA messages from this book socially by going to
https://aha.pub/DoYouSpeakPatient

Scan the QR code or use this link to watch the section videos and more on this section topic:
https://aha.pub/DoYouSpeakPatientSVs

Section VII

Eliminate Barriers Now

Medical professionals do extraordinary things for people in the course of normal days. Enhancing health and life quality as well as saving lives is standard expectation. High stress tolerance among the profession is the norm. But problems begin to arise when an inefficient healthcare system creates barriers to performance of this extraordinary work. More simply stated, healthcare systems and tools should facilitate the delivery of our very best care to patients, and should make it increasingly simple for patients to seek the care they need. Unfortunately, that is often not what happens, and these systemic barriers become a source of distress for professional and patient alike.

As the medical industry matures, many barriers pop up in the healthcare system that get in the way of us delivering quality health care to patients. The barriers often prove more stressful than the job of saving lives. Staffing issues, physical resources, paperwork, archaic procedures, insurance prior authorization, financial difficulties for patient or professional, and profound inefficiencies in electronic recordkeeping have caused many medical professionals to burn out, preventing delivery of optimal health care.

A great deal of collaboration, cooperation, and coordination needs to happen to rise above these challenges and ensure no additional stress is placed on either medical professionals or patients. That way, patients can have higher chances of optimized recovery.

Healthcare systems that prioritize an optimal environment for medical professionals to work with and for patients is what we need. At present, it is too common that competing priorities deemphasize the basic core function of hospitals and clinics, which is patient care. When a decision must be made, it is clear in a high-functioning system that the needs of the patient come first. Simply stated, the primary job of the medical professional is to take care of the person right in front of them.

105

Medical professionals are great at what they do best -- enhancing health and saving lives. This purpose-driven work is not the source of distress. More commonly, navigating system inefficiencies creates it. #CredibleMedicalProfessional

_____

_____

_____

106

Medical professionals need to be able to work in hospitals that will meet the needs of every patient. When system constraints result in patients not seeking needed care, outcomes are profoundly compromised. #CredibleMedicalProfessional

_____

_____

_____

107

A sound healthcare system can make a difference in how medical professionals deliver quality care to patients. How does your healthcare system impact your community? #CredibleMedicalProfessional

_____

_____

_____

108

Highly trained and dedicated medical professionals can take care of patients the way they deserve to be taken care of in multiple different clinical settings. #CredibleMedicalProfessional

_____

_____

_____

109

There are endless possibilities for medical professionals to help prevent patients' poor health. However, too much bureaucratic work can get in the way. What are the top 3 inefficiencies that create barriers in your work? #CredibleMedicalProfessional

_____

_____

_____

110

Patient care gets compromised when medical professionals have an inefficient system where there's a workforce shortage and discontent. How do you deal with these barriers? #CredibleMedicalProfessional

_____

_____

_____

111

Patient care is often a life-or-death situation.
In this case, which barriers are acceptable?
#CredibleMedicalProfessional

_____

_____

_____

112

The world saw the ineffectiveness of public health
delivery during the COVID-19 pandemic. There was not
enough personnel, finances, or technology to support
the demand for patient care, and there were many
disparities. #CredibleMedicalProfessional

_____

_____

_____

113

The global shortage of medical professionals needs to be addressed, as it puts health professionals in distress, and patients at risk of harm.
#CredibleMedicalProfessional

_____

_____

_____

114

Medical professionals need to balance healthcare quality and efficiency by allocating limited medications and resources to sustain the workforce and address patient needs simultaneously. #CredibleMedicalProfessional

_____

_____

_____

115

Applications of technology to medical care could best be applied to eliminating barriers. When technology application makes workflows less efficient, it is counterproductive to patient care. #CredibleMedicalProfessional

_____

_____

_____

116

Technological advances have the potential to transform health care, but too often they create confusion and a potential for harm. What are the most promising technology opportunities in your field of medicine? #CredibleMedicalProfessional

_____

_____

_____

117

Scheduling conflicts and logistics can result in care compromises. Where do you see quality and safety risks emerge in your environment?
#CredibleMedicalProfessional

_____

_____

_____

118

Medical professionals need reliable systems to track patients' conditions in order to effectively use data in predicting demand for care. Data analytics are often ineffective or are not used to guide treatment decisions.
#CredibleMedicalProfessional

_____

_____

_____

119

Optimizing access points in healthcare eliminates emergency room bottlenecks or mix-ups between urgent and routine care. Many systems have inadequately diversified access strategies to meet the needs of diverse populations. #CredibleMedicalProfessional

_____

_____

_____

120

Diversification of access points allows patients to receive the right care by the right professional at the right time. #CredibleMedicalProfessional

_____

_____

_____

121

Medical professional teams must coordinate to adequately meet the needs of chronically ill patients with complex medical needs. Successful healthcare system reforms will assure robust opportunities for collaboration. #CredibleMedicalProfessional

---

122

Medical professionals need to work with the healthcare system to bring care to people where they are, and not the other way around. This will remove stress on both sides and not limit health services. #CredibleMedicalProfessional

---

123

When access to medical professionals is as limited as it is today, every departure from the field compounds the crisis. Professional health and well-being must be prioritized to prevent deterioration of patient access. #CredibleMedicalProfessional

_____

_____

_____

124

To reduce burnout, emphasis is often put on mindfulness, self-care, and relationship building, but the real gains come from improving the efficiency of the care environment. #CredibleMedicalProfessional

_____

_____

_____

125

The healthcare system should provide workplace support and minimize long work hours for medical professionals to thrive and avoid burnout. #CredibleMedicalProfessional

---

126

The perfect health system would enable medical professionals to deliver their best at all times, helping make life better for the patients they serve. #CredibleMedicalProfessional

---

Share the AHA messages from this book socially by going to
https://aha.pub/DoYouSpeakPatient

Scan the QR code or use this link to watch the section videos and more on this section topic:
https://aha.pub/DoYouSpeakPatientSVs

Section VIII

Conclusion

It is in the medical professional's best interest for the general population to be healthier. People are more productive and more able when they are well.

Medical professionals can achieve this by being credible and deeply caring for their fellow humans with empathy, trustworthiness, integrity, and respect, particularly when they are ill.

It is important for medical professionals to show respect in patient care, display integrity in applying knowledge and expertise, exemplify trustworthiness in the workplace, and demonstrate empathy to patients.

A credible medical professional is someone who has these qualities and refuses to put his/her position, accomplishments, titles, and accolades before the patient's needs. The credible physician serves others -- fellow humans -- and truly takes care of those in need across all dimensions of wellness.

Adequately and empathetically delivering care for each patient is one step closer to healthier individuals and stronger communities. This is our contribution to the world. This is why we save lives.

This book concludes with this section, which answers how powerful it is when medical professionals have credibility. Credible medical professionals also have healthy, lasting relationships with colleagues in the medical field and, most especially, with patients.

If you seem to have lost your passion somewhere along your medical journey, this book will help you get back to what drives you to do what you once swore to do, and to deliver the job that you're supposed to do -- in service to others. Make your own additions, and customize the AHA messages to your professional life.

127

It is in the medical professional's best interest for the general population to be healthier. People are more productive and happier when they are healthy. #CredibleMedicalProfessional

_____

_____

_____

128

Healthy individuals help communities prosper,
thereby contributing to society's progress. Quality
of life is multidimensional and transformative.
#CredibleMedicalProfessional

_____

_____

_____

129

Integrity, respect, trustworthiness, and empathy
-- all these increase a person's credibility, which is
an important attribute for medical professionals.
#CredibleMedicalProfessional

_____

_____

_____

130

Increasing your credibility is an important part of growing as a professional. It's not just about what you do, but why you do what you do. Intent is one thing, but impact is another. How do you assess your impact? #CredibleMedicalProfessional

----

131

As medical practitioners, you should have empathy with your knowledge and expertise. That way, the various treatment options at your disposal can be used more effectively. #CredibleMedicalProfessional

_____

_____

_____

132

The patient has decision rights regarding their care, but you need to set the context about what that decision means. A #CredibleMedicalProfessional understands patient needs to advance their life quality.

_____

_____

_____

133

A break in integrity begins to erode internal credibility and is a risk for burnout. Behavior consistent with values maintains integrity and minimizes this risk. #CredibleMedicalProfessional

_____

134

When a patient puts their health and life in your hands, there has to be a significant level of trust and respect. #CredibleMedicalProfessional

_____

135

Respect is an important aspect in patient care. Show respect to everybody, including your colleagues and subordinates, because it drives quality and patient safety. #CredibleMedicalProfessional

---

136

With even minor disrespect, medical professionals may find themselves in hostile work environments that are detrimental to the patient's condition. #CredibleMedicalProfessional

---

137

Strive to be a trusted and credible medical professional committed to providing outstanding healthcare and service by caring for your patients and colleagues as fellow human beings. #CredibleMedicalProfessional

_____

_____

_____

138

When your relationships with patients are built on trust and empathy, you help facilitate cooperation. Gaining cooperation means you get to open up opportunities to improve the patient's overall health. #CredibleMedicalProfessional

_____

_____

_____

139

Go back to why you got into the medical profession in the first place. How well do your current behaviors serve that purpose? #CredibleMedicalProfessional

_____

_____

_____

140

Being a medical professional puts you in a position to serve others and take care of your fellow humans. That's a tremendous value to this world. #CredibleMedicalProfessional

_____

_____

_____

Appendix

All proceeds will be used to provide new opportunities for students to pursue education as medical professionals by supporting the growth of the University of North Carolina at Wilmington Health Equity for Aspiring Leaders Endowed Scholarship (HEAL Scholarship).

About the Author

Doc Philip Brown formerly served as EVP, Chief Physician Executive at New Hanover Regional Medical Center and Chief Community Impact Officer at Novant Health with a proven track record of building high performing teams. He believes the healthcare industry needs radical reinvention, and that we should focus on understanding different needs, and then create opportunities for all people to reach their highest level of health.

Dr. Brown's ability to bring simplicity out of chaos in order to help lead organizations and individuals to accountable action is particularly needed in today's environment. When we are inundated with facts and data points that can be and are spun to obscure truth, creating clarity requires both quantitative and qualitative information. His transformational leadership is effective because he is willing to listen, hear, and understand diverse perspectives through connection and earned trust.

Creating environments where teams can innovate courageously, bolstered by a resiliency that makes the potential of failure a stepping stone rather than a barrier, is a modern challenge to effective leadership. Dr. Brown's methods make it possible to amplify all voices so it becomes easier to identify common goals, dream bigger visions of what can be accomplished together, and create aligned action (not just plans) for achieving amazing results. Through deep connection and trust, teams can develop the resiliency that allows this kind of breakthrough performance.

Above all, Dr. Brown is a doctor deeply concerned about the health and life quality of his patients and colleagues.

THiNKaha has created AHAthat for you to share content from this book.

➲ Share each AHA message socially: **https://aha.pub/DoYouSpeakPatient**

➲ Share additional content: **https://AHAthat.com**

➲ Info on authoring: **https://AHAthat.com/Author**

CPSIA information can be obtained
at www.ICGtesting.com
Printed in the USA
BVHW090018280423
663158BV00019B/751